Dear Lord,

With Love,

Gloria

Tender Moments with God

1-11-04

Vinie

Numbers 6:24-26

In Jesus love + ministry,

Gloria Coffeet

i

Dear Lord,

With Love,

Gloria

Tender Moments with God

Gloria Coffelt

Dear Lord, With Love, Gloria

Copyright© 2001
By Gloria Coffelt

Library of Congress Control Number: 2001119048
ISBN   0-9714251-0-8

Cover Design: Jeff Hatcher

Published by

*G*race *P*ublishing
1025 Dove Run Rd. # 108, Lexington, KY 40502

Printed in the United States by:
Morris Publishing – 3212 East Hwy. 30
Kearney, NE 68847

Contents

Short Stories

Conversations With The Lord

Forgiveness

Help In A Time of Trouble

Journeying

In The Palm of His Hand

v

Understanding Myself

Who Is Jehovah?

Dedication

This book is dedicated to my heavenly Father, Jesus Christ and the Holy Spirit, I give glory, honor and praise. Without You magnificent Savior, there would be no book! It was Your gift to me. Without Your everlasting love, I would have nothing to write about. Thank you for the inspiration.

With Love,

Gloria

About the Title

  *F*our or five years ago, my Heavenly Father seemed to be prompting me to call Him Lord. There are so many names for our Lord since He is a multifaceted God and let me say right here and now, I love them all. But, Lord, for me seemed to be "just right."

  Then one day I was reading in Ezekiel 6 from the Zondervan Amplified Bible and it pointed out that Lord in the Bible occurs around 5,000 times. The footnote also explained God uses it more often than any other important word in the Bible; and that "Lord" becomes the most essential term in any language for the welfare of any person. We must accept Him as Lord of our lives.

Foreward

Gloria Coffelt's prayers and stories ring with the passion of a soul who, once she really found it, has not lost her "first love"—Jesus Christ. Her writing expresses her driven mission for others to experience that same "Jesus relationship" that brings the joy and spiritual peace she knows. Her ministry through these words from the heart is worship.

--The Editor

Acknowledgments

With warm gratitude, I offer a most grateful heart. I know your prayers sustained me when the task seemed insurmountable:

Anita Alcorn, for consistently demonstrating a servant's heart. For supporting me through all my delays. For helping the vision become a reality. I'm most grateful for your fasting and praying on my behalf, for the many times you've dropped me a note, or called to encourage me. You were my first friend to read my manuscript and encourage me to "publish the book."

Lavelle Brown and Ednamae Compton, whose friendship has blessed my life beyond measure. Your fervent prayers have brought blessing after blessing to me. You never gave up on the book.

Martha Hudson, my precious friend, who has never given up on me. My treasured friend through thick and thin, who kept the vision burning brightly even when it became dim to me. Thanks for not letting me give up.

Diana Smith, my new friend. It's been awesome to experience your willingness to allow the Holy Spirit to flow through you with intensity and incredible encouragement for me, to "publish the book".

To Gary, my husband and best friend, whose continual encouragement, support and prayers kept me moving toward the finish line. Without your help typing, editing and designing this book it would still be a dream in the making.

To, my beloved sons, Scott, Jeff and Tony, my blessed encouragers who always asked about the book and believed it would be a reality. Thanks guys, you three are my earthly sunshine.

To Jake and Jensen, my precious twin grandchildren. Thanks for sharing your world with me to inspire me for a children's book "Just a Little Talk With Jesus." You make me smile way deep in my soul. I love you.

Introduction

*I*t is my prayer that by reading "Dear Lord, With Love, Gloria", the Holy Love Letter from God, His Holy Word, will become alive and very personal to you. It is my desire, that if it is for the first time or the hundredth time, the realization that He loves you so much He can't take His eyes off you, will penetrate your heart.

*M*y prayer is that by sharing some personal times with our Abba Father, a desire hidden deep in your spirit will awaken, and you too will cry out to Jesus, "Help me fall in love with You, as no other, help me desire an intimate relationship with You."

*I*saiah 29:13, "Wherefore the Lord said, Forasmuch as this people draw near me with their mouth, And with their lips do honor me, But have removed their heart far from me, And their fear towards me is taught by the precept of men." (KJV). That verse described me so well for so many years. I had asked Jesus into my heart as a very young child. I believed and I received, but I failed to develop an intimate relationship with Jesus. I feared God and wanted to be a good person. I attended church Sunday morning and

His holy word will come alive.

Sunday night and most Wednesday evenings. I was saved but I walked in reason and logic and was trying to "do the right thing." The holy rest and peace of Jesus eluded me. I was saved but lost in tradition and religion. For me it was all about following the rules, not a relationship. I left out grace and mercy.

I knew little about the Holy Spirit. I knew He lived within me but I failed to get acquainted with Him, to allow the Holy Spirit to take me into the presence of God. I didn't allow Him to reveal to *"trying* me the things of God. I accepted the *to do* supernatural power that it took to save *the* me and to have a "born again" *right* experience, but I rarely, if ever, called *thing"* on the supernatural power to transform me. I kept trying to do it by a form of religion, trying "to be good". I heard the Word, I tried to follow the Word, but I left out the Power of the Word.

I didn't realize that I needed to be continually filled with the Holy Spirit. I have learned that if we censor any part of His Word, we're not walking in the light. We must accept the whole Bible, not just part of it. By cutting out an ongoing relationship with the Holy Spirit, the Power is unplugged.

One day I stopped at some verses in Psalms 139:16-18, "You saw me before I was born and scheduled each day of my life before I began to breathe. Every day was recorded in Your Book! How precious it is, Lord, to realize that You are thinking about me CONSTANTLY! I can't even count how many times a day Your thoughts turn toward me. And when I awaken in the morning, you are still thinking of me!" (CLB). Please pause for a moment and ponder just how incredible that is. Please stop and ask the Holy Spirit to reveal to you deep in the recesses of your soul that this is truth. He does love you so much He is thinking about you constantly.

After the Holy Spirit drew me into confession of being lukewarm, having idols in my life, and instructing me to repent and turn my eyes on Jesus, He led me to a remarkable verse in the Bible. It was Psalm 24:3-4a, "Who shall ascend into the hill of the Lord or who shall stand in His holy place? He that hath clean hands, and a pure heart." (KJV). I desperately wanted clean hands and a pure heart. I wanted to ascend into the hill of the Lord. I desired to be in His presence. I wanted my affections on things above, not on things of this earth (Col. 3:2). I prayed to have the eyes of my heart opened, I prayed to have the veil removed

He loves you so much.

9

from my eyes, and I prayed to have a willing heart, Psalm 119:32, "I will (not merely walk), but run the way of Your commandments, when you give me a heart that is willing." (AMP). I ASKED the Holy Spirit to plow up my heart and make it fallow ground. I found myself continually humming under my breath and singing in my car, "Change my heart, oh, God, make it ever new. Change my heart, oh, God, may I be like You."

Help me fall in love with Jesus.

I noticed that I began to experience a "joy unspeakable" in my heart even though in my earthly circumstances the storms were gathering ground-speeds that were insurmountable. There was peace in my spirit and I entered His "rest". I continued to call out to the "Holy Spirit" who resided in me, "Fill me with Your love, help me fall in love with Jesus, and help me to love as God loves, with an agape love."

One day, I began driving the hour and a half distance to work. I couldn't wait to turn on praise music, express my love to Jesus, and bask in His love. Just before I arrived at my destination, something unusual happened. I stopped hearing the music in my car and my heart began to make it's own melody; the words of adoration were engraved deep in my heart. They were no longer just words. It was as if my entire being was worshiping Him. I longed to see His face. What took place next is almost too sacred to talk about, but I feel led of the Holy Spirit to share. SUDDENLY, it was as if heaven just opened up and love, divine love spilled over into my car. It filled up with the glory of His presence, the sweet essence of my Lord. I've never experienced such love in my entire life. The experience was so holy, I believe, that earthly words are inadequate to describe it. I just know I shall never be the same. The power of His love was so great I couldn't receive it all. I had to put out my hand asking Him to withhold--I couldn't contain it all. My affections were changed; they were on things above and no longer things on earth. I knew He had called me out to share the Word, to encourage others to fall in love with Him.

Divine love spilled over into my car.

God's Word says in Acts 10:34 that He shows no partially and is not a respecter of persons. He has no favorites. He loves each of His children equally. What He does for one, He will and can do for all.

Since my experience, there have been many trials and staggering realities in my search for truth, but the pursuit of Jesus has never dimmed. I keep pressing on to see His face. Since that time, the Holy Spirit has encouraged me to write my own love notes back to God in response to His Holy

Word, His Love Letter. The Bible is now alive to me. It's no longer musty words, written long ago. It's a Love Letter that envelops me like a warm blanket.

*M*y beloved friends, test everything you hear by God's Word. Do not accept any teaching **Test everything you hear by God's Word.** without asking for scripture to back it up. Do not allow anyone to add to or censor what the Holy Word has told us. Appeal to the Holy Spirit who lives within you to reveal truth to you. The truth will set you free. My beloved friends do not be afraid of the Holy Spirit. You can't just read about the Holy Spirit, you must experience Him. Remember, he is part of the Godhead, the holy trinity. You won't understand God's Holy Word, without the Holy Spirit. It will seem foolish to you. (I Cor. 2:14)

*A*fter having the direction of the Holy Spirit to write down my own love notes to God, I wasn't quite sure what to do with them. So I placed them in my cedar chest to save for my children and grandchildren. I prayed over them and gave them to God to use for His honor and His glory. I told Him if He wanted them shared with His children He would have to show me how.

*S*ome time passed, and one of our Lord's precious saints moved to our small lake town from

New York state. She was a writer and English-as-a Second Language teacher. We not only shared a love for writing but also the same first name. I shall never forget the time I opened my door and there she stood, expressing that she felt God wanted her to edit my prayers for me. God was certainly at work. I was excited to think just perhaps, God would use my prayers. At

Our Savior placed a call on my heart.

the time she began editing for me she was traveling by plane to visit her ailing Dad in Minnesota. She sent me a sweet note expressing how appropriate it was to be editing my work thirty thousand feet in the clouds; that God was ministering to her through those prayers. God is so good! Right after that our Savior placed a call on my heart to go to Russia. A group I was representing decided to have my prayers transcribed in Russian so they could be shared with the ladies at the conference. God was working!

*T*he next confirmation came when a precious friend called and said she felt God was telling her to upfront publishing costs because the manuscript needed to be published here in the United States. She asked to remain anonymous, explaining to me she was storing up treasures in heaven—not on earth—by being obedient. *I*t was so exciting to see the hand of God moving.

*T*hen came the day I called out to God about the cover. After all, it was His book, and I wanted

The time was glorious with the Lord.

to continue letting Him lead all the way. The Lord called me into a season of fasting and praying. He provided the opportunity for me to fly to a beach area for a few days. The time was glorious with the Lord-- praying, worshiping, and reading His Word. The last afternoon I was there, I decided to leave my room and walk on the beach. There, I met four adorable children and chatted with their precious parents who were about the age of my adult children. We became acquainted, and I shared my dilemma of finding someone to design my book cover. The couple invited me to have breakfast with them the next morning before my plane left. It was then that I learned that Jeff was a graphic artist and worked with several Christian publications. He would be more than glad to design my book cover.

*O*n the way home, I just closed my eyes and praised the Lord! It was awesome how he had found me so many midwives to birth the book, "Dear Lord, With Love, Gloria." I prayed a prayer of thanks-giving, "Father, it is Your work, and You've sent Your finest laborers. My heartfelt gratitude and praise goes to You."

So dear readers, I tenderly place this new baby in your hands. My prayer is that God's anointing will flow forth, penetrating your heart. The purpose of this introduction is to allow you to see what Jesus does with ordinary men and women, by His extraordinary power. The book is to encourage you to "seek His face" and to get acquainted with the Holy Spirit. By the end of

"precious sons and daughters of Jesus"

this book, precious sons and daughters of Jesus (I borrowed this phrase from my dear beloved pastor friend from Africa, Dr. Zerubbabel Ebangit) I pray you too, will continue to journey with me and together we'll continue our journey of falling in love with Jesus. I am now beginning my second work, "May I See Them Through Your Eyes?" It's a journal about God in the marketplace. May I end with a quote from A.W. Tozer, "Love and faith are at home in the mystery of the Godhead. Let reason kneel in reverence outside."

In Jesus' Love and mine too,

*G*loria

The Great I Am

As I walked throughout my neighborhood,
I cried to the Lord;
I pleaded for Him to send me a message.
I continued reciting to Him all the stories
I had heard of angels appearing to people
And giving them a
Message from Heaven.

The farther I walked the more excited
I became. I pleaded, "Father, just one angel.
Please send an angel to me with
A message from You."
I continued to plead, until
I was almost back home again.
An hour had passed as my home was in sight,
I sighed sadly, "I don't guess You are going
To send me an Angel with a message."

Instantly, I heard His voice, from deep
Within my spirit.
"My child I have been talking to you.
Would you rather me send an angel
Instead of myself?"
Very embarrassed, I exclaimed,
"Oh, no Father! Forgive me.
All I want is to be in Your presence and
Hear Your precious voice."

Illuminating: Our Father wants to
speak with us. We must get still before Him
and open our hearts and listen.

Psalm 39:13: Spare me, Lord! Let me recover and be filled with happiness again before my death. (CLB)

Psalm 39:7: And so, Lord, my only hope is in you. (CLB)
Psalm 56:8: You have taken account of my wanderings; Put my tears in Your bottle. Are they not in Your book? (CLB)

Girlfriends

Easter Sunday is always such a special time for me. I feel the excitement of Spring, tulips in bloom, and everywhere I look is a soft lush green. But much more than that, it's an awesome celebration of my Savior rising from the dead and providing a way for me to have eternal life. But today I was sad. I had moved to another city just a month before from a house that had been home to me for twenty-three years. A marriage that I had spent half of my life in was over; a different house, a different town and a new life.

$\mathcal{M}$y son had come home from college to go to church with me and after lunch, he and Duke the boxer headed back to college. The house seemed lonely and empty.

I decided to go for a walk. I put on dark sunglasses and as I walked I could feel the tears stinging my eyes and flowing from under my dark glasses. I felt so mixed up and so alone. I had resigned from my career a couple of years earlier to devote more time to my family and to follow a call I felt God had placed on my life; a call to serve Him in ministry. With the new move also came a new job.

I felt God had placed a call on my life. The new job wasn't working out and I kept praying, asking God to help me. Deep in my spirit, I could feel the still, small whisper that I knew belonged to my Lord, and He said, " My child what can I do for you?" I sobbed, "Jesus, I need girlfriends. I need girlfriends that love you as much as I do. Father, I miss the ladies I prayed with. I've been praying with them for years and there is such a bond there. I need another prayer team." I looked at my watch and it was around 3:45 P.M. I decided to head back home and get ready to go to the worship service.

I didn't realize until arriving that this particular service started at 6:08 P.M and was focused on attracting college students and other young adults; I was amazed at all the youthful faces I saw. I felt quite comfortable though, since I'm the mother of three young adult men. The place was packed already and as I looked for an empty space, I noticed close to the front of the church an available seat. As I took the seat, I saw the warm smile of the lady sitting next to me. She and her friend appeared to be about my age. They introduced themselves to me as Chris and her friend Kathy.

The worship service was wonderful and I could feel my spirit rise as my praise rose to Jesus. About half way through the service, Chris leaned toward me and said, "I'm a widow and today I invited my friend Kathy over for dinner after church. Somewhere between 3:30 and 4:00 P.M., the Lord spoke to me in my spirit and said, 'Set another plate.' She continued on, when *"Could the plate be for you?"* my friend came by to pick me up, she asked whom the other plate was for and I told her a stranger." Chris then looked me in the eye and smiled ever so gently, and said, "Could the plate be for you?" I knew that it was! Yes, my Lord is faithful. He had found me girlfriends that loved Jesus as much as I did. I accepted and had a wonderful time at her house. It was as if we had always known each other.

I shared with Chris how very much I missed my prayer team and she graciously invited me to her prayer team. It consisted of about fifteen people who had been meeting for ten years every Wednesday night. They have potluck dinner together at each other's homes and then pair off in groups and pray for each other's children. The following Wednesday night, I met to pray with the team and they welcomed me with open arms. My spirit joined with their spirit.

*O*ur Heavenly Father is so faithful and responds to our every need. In Psalm 50:15-16, God says, "Trust me in your times of trouble, and I will rescue you, and you will give me glory." (NLT). He

All my tears I trust to Jesus.

told me in Psalm 56:8 that he stored all my tears in a bottle, and that he records all my sorrows in His Book. A few months later, my new friend Chris went to Israel to study at the Hebrew University. She brought back to me a tiny souvenir, an official "tear bottle," its purpose being a storage place for tears. The bottle was about two inches tall. My new friend explained that it was small because she didn't want me to have very many tears to shed. All my tears I trust to Jesus, knowing He will rescue me and I will give the honor and the glory to Him.

*M*y praise and glory to Him is Psalm 57:7-11, "My heart is steadfast, O God, my heart is steadfast; I will sing, yes, I will sing praises! Awake, my glory! Awake, harp and lyre! I will awaken the dawn. I will give thanks to You, O Lord, among the peoples; I will sing praises to You among the nations. For Your loving kindness is great to the heavens And Your Truth to the clouds. Be exalted above the heavens, O God; Let Your glory be above all the earth." (NAS). And Amen. All Glory to God.

I Kings 19: 12: And after the earthquake there was a fire, but the Lord was not in the fire. And after the fire there was the sound of a gentle whisper. (NLT)

John 10:4: After he has gathered his own flock, he walks ahead of them, and they follow him because they recognize his voice. (NLT)

The Love Exchange

As I was boarding the plane for a business trip, my mind was crowded with expectations of the meeting I would be entering when I arrived at my destination. I had just received a promotion to Regional Manager and the whirlwind of budgets, hiring new people and meeting quotas was more than just a passing thought. I felt I was well prepared for the meeting, and had on purpose placed a book in my briefcase called "The Love Exchange". It was my favorite book in the whole world. I was looking forward to some quiet time on the flight to once again savor the pages and let them penetrate my heart. The book was written by a gifted author who gently reminded me of the lavish love our Savior has for us. I had read it many times, but it seemed I gave away every copy I purchased. The last time I gave away my copy, I was very saddened when I learned that it was out of print when I tried to re-order at the Christian bookstore. I had learned about the book through my dear pastor. When I shared with him that I had even written the author trying to get a copy, I remember so well that he unlocked his study and to my surprise, came out with another copy, placed it in my hand, and said, "Don't give this one away, there are no more." I treasured the newfound copy and looked forward tremendously to once again devouring the message of this book. I had already planned on having no conversation with the other passengers. I was on a mission and that mission was to once again re-read my favorite book.

"Don't give this one away."

As I boarded the plane, I noticed that a very beautiful elderly woman was in my seat. Beside her was an empty seat by the window. I decided to take it and not say anything, hoping that seat was hers. Before the plane took off, she touched my arm and began to ask me questions. I could tell she wanted to talk. She had no idea I was on a mission to once again cuddle with my very favorite book. I decided to chat with her for a little while and learned she did not have children and she was eighty years old. Big tears filled her gorgeous blue eyes as she whispered, "I have just discovered I have cancer. I'm flying to Oklahoma City to meet my nephew who is a doctor. He will take care of me."

*M*y heart went out to her. By the time the plane taxied for take off we both were settled in and the conversation was flowing smoothly. I quietly asked her if she knew Jesus. She hesitated but then replied, "Yes, I do." I then asked her if she realized how much He loved her. Again she hesitated but replied, "I think so."

"Give her the book."

*A*s we visited and shared our favorite books, Broadway plays, colors, and a bonding passion for chocolate, I heard deep in my spirit a still, small voice saying, "Give her the book." I ignored it, thinking that my Lord would surely not ask me to give her my precious book! Instead, I reached in my purse and pulled out a valentine, since it was Valentine's Day. I wrote an encouraging message on the card, handed it to her and assured her I wouldn't forget to pray. She was grateful and once again, we settled down, she dozing and I pondering. I glanced over at her, and she looked so helpless, so beautiful and so childlike. Then once again, in my spirit, I heard, gently but firmly, "Give her the book." Well, I just knew that my Father would not be saying that to me. I shifted in my seat. Then once again, a little louder than a whisper but still very gently, He said, "My child, give her the book." Tears of joy sprang into my eyes, as I recognized my Father's voice. No one calls me "My child" except my heavenly Father.

Just as we were landing she woke up and I gave her the book! I explained to her that God told me to give her the book because He loved her so much and He had inspired the book's author to write about His extravagant love for His children. She clutched it to her breast and her eyes danced. She told me she felt so special. I kissed her goodbye on the cheek and she said, "I hope to see you again, but if not here on earth, I'll see you in Heaven."

Tears of joy sprang into my eyes.

As I left the plane, I said, "Thank you Father, for trusting me with your special child. Thank you for calling me "My child"; I recognized my Father's voice. Now Father, let's talk about finding me another book, okay? You know it has a blue cover, and it's called "The Love Exchange." Do you think you could use your connections and find me another one? Father are you listening?"

Luke 15:7: There's more joy in heaven over one sinner's rescued life than over ninety-nine good people in no need of rescue. (The Message)

Martha

Although it's been fourteen years, I remember as if it were yesterday, the first time I met Martha. I was an insurance sales representative who provided benefit information to school employees. Martha was a schoolteacher. I was at the board office to review Martha's insurance benefits with her. We were concluding our visit, when I heard our Savior speak to my heart and say, "My child, more than disability insurance, Martha needs Me." I silently whispered back, "I know Jesus, but I'm not ready. I need more training." Once again, in my spirit I heard Him so quietly and gently say, "My child, the time is now. I'll never leave or forsake you." I still remember so well nervously clearing my throat and saying weakly,

"Martha, I would love to share with you about the greatest friend I've ever known."

As I began sharing with Martha, my heart was beating so fast in my ears that I couldn't even hear what I was saying. I did notice *I need more training.* that her expression was not changing, and she looked very perplexed. She politely excused herself, and as I was clearing my things away, I expressed my concern to the heavenly Father, "Oh, Father what if she complains to the superintendent about me?" Once, again, in my spirit, I heard Him say, "I love you my child, I will never leave or forsake you."

Since I was at the board office for the entire summer reviewing benefits with teachers, I saw Martha on a couple of other occasions. Once, I asked her if she'd like to go get pizza. She accepted and while we were eating, she commented laughingly on my necklace.

It was a tiny gold cross and chain that I had worn for many years. She began to share that when I first started to explain her benefits to her on the first day we met, the lights in the room were dancing off my cross necklace, making it impossible for her to see my face. She said the cross seemed to be so large that it was all she could see. Then, when I had *It was a tiny gold cross.*

begun to speak of Jesus, she felt this was too coincidental.

Several years passed and every summer I was scheduled back to this same school district to review benefits with the teachers. Every summer, Martha allowed me to share with her another piece of the redemption story of Jesus Christ. I continued to share with her about how much Jesus loved her; that He loved her so much He couldn't take His eyes off her.

We became friends. A couple of times a year Martha would visit me when she was shopping where I lived.

Nine years went by. We talked on the phone every few months, and the conversations were almost entirely about our Lord and Savior and how much He loved her. Martha had a lot of head knowledge about God, but the heart knowledge and the relationship were missing. Sometimes I would become discouraged, and share with our Father, "I don't think she's ever going to ask you into her heart." But He would tell me, "Be still, my child, I'm still in control."

"Be still my child."

Then on September 23, 1996, my birthday, a miraculous thing happened. I was preparing to leave on a mission trip to Russia. My doorbell rang, and

31

there stood Martha. She was ready to ask Jesus into her heart.

Our God is so faithful. I explained to Martha that a big party was going on in heaven just because of her. The angels were celebrating, Martha's "new birth" day. For me, this was the most special birthday ever.

Martha and I now can be friends for eternity. I celebrate my earthly birthday every fall and Martha celebrates with me her "born again" birthday. Together we celebrate our sisterhood in Jesus Christ.

Luke 14:23: And the Lord said unto the servant, Go out into the highways and hedges, and compel *them* to come in, that my house may be filled. (KJV)

Ephesians 6:18: Pray at all times and on every occasion in the power of the Holy Spirit. Stay alert and be persistent in your prayers for all Christians everywhere. (NLT)

Ephesians 6:10-13: A final word: Be strong with the Lord's mighty power. Put on all of God's armor, so that you will be able to stand firm against all strategies and tricks of the Devil. For we are not fighting against people made of flesh and blood, but against the evil rulers and authorities of the unseen world, against those mighty powers of darkness who rule this world, and against wicked spirits in the heavenly realms. (NLT)

Zechariah 10:2: Household gods give false advice, **fortune-tellers** predict only lies, and interpreters of dreams pronounce comfortless falsehoods. (NLT)

Isaiah 45:22: I have swept away your sins like the morning mists. I have scattered your offences, like the clouds. Oh, return to me, for I have paid the price to set you free. (NLT)

Isaiah 6:8: Whom shall I send? And who will go for us? And I said, Here am I send me. (CLB)

Psalms 140:16: You saw me before I was born and scheduled each day of my life before I began to breathe. Every day was recorded in your Book! (CLB)

God's Warm Surprise

It's Saturday, a warm, sweet July day. I have one big project in mind. I love Saturdays. There's time for that extra cup of coffee or a leisurely phone call; but not today. Today, I'm cleaning the garage and I'm excited about it. Well, maybe excited isn't exactly the word I'm looking for--- maybe "joyfully resigned" would be a better description. My plans are carefully laid out and woe to any distractions today; no time to hear about a neighbor's son's wedding, or smell the flowers. TODAY I'M CLEANING THE GARAGE.

While I'm making good progress, my mind wanders as I thank God for a new friend who has entered my life. My son, Tony, is fourteen and changing school districts. That means new friends for him and therefore possibly new friends for me, too.

My son has made a new friend in the new school system he is attending. I'm feeling very grateful for the new friend's mother *"Bake Susan a cake."* picking up my son, from school so that he may attend a golf tournament with her son. (The company I work for has me scheduled out of state for a business meeting.) God does provide for his children. I love being a child of the King.

I notice that I'm about halfway through the project I had dreaded for days and I'm feeling really good about my progress. Without any warning, the thought is pressed on my mind, "Bake Susan (the mother of Tony's new friend) a cake." Oh, no, what am I thinking: BAKE HER A CAKE. Now? Surely not! I'm in the middle of cleaning my garage. After all, somewhere, haven't I read that, cleanliness is next to Godliness? Okay, so my mother said that, instead of God. But it still sounds like a good idea to me. If I stop in the middle of this project to bake a cake, I won't get finished today. Once again, a gentle nudging within my spirit whispers, "Bake Susan a cake." Once again I push it aside, reminding myself, that I'd sent a thank you note and purchased her a nice green plant to express my gratitude.

*O*kay, someday I'll bake her a cake, but not today. Today I must stay focused and clean the garage. I reach over to turn off my praise music, and as I continue cleaning, the sweetest voice I've ever heard, yes, it is a voice that could stop the birds from singing, says "My child, bake Susan a cake." This voice is coming from deep within my spirit. There is only one person who calls me His child and that is God, my heavenly Father. I look up toward heaven and exclaim, "I know You dear Father, know what You are doing. It doesn't make sense to me but I will just trust You and obey."

It doesn't make sense to me.

*A*s I wash my hands and lay out the ingredients, I know this cake has to be special. I search in my freezer for black walnuts I have been saving for a special occasion. I searched for my special recipe of dark fudge frosting. The cake recipe is a special chocolate cake that was handed down to me by my mother-in-law. I know since this cake is so special that it needs to be delivered while the cake is still warm.

Just as I put the finishing touches on the icing, my husband walks into the kitchen. He's surprised I'm baking a cake when he knows that just a short time earlier I was working on the garage. I answer with, "God told me to." He offers to drive me to the new friend's house.

As I ring her doorbell, she answers the door all smiles, "How did you know it was my birthday? Who told you?" I reply, "I didn't know. *God told me to.* But God did. Perhaps He was on His balcony in heaven and called out, 'Children, today is your sister's birthday. Who will bake a cake for her?' I guess I was listening and was honored to bake the cake."

Thank you Lord, for allowing me to be a part of Your blessing.

Ephesians 4:32: Be ye kind one to another, tenderhearted, forgiving one another, even as God for Christ's sake hath forgiven you.   (KJV)

Titus 3:2: To speak evil of no man, to be no brawlers, but gentle, shewing all meekness unto all men. (KJV)

Feelings That Are Hurt

Dear Lord,

Oh, perfect and loving Father, quiet my spirit. Help me to have a loving, forgiving spirit when someone has spoken unkindly of me or has hurt my feelings. Help me release it to You, Lord, without hesitation.

Father, You tell us in Your Word in Psalm 66:18, "If I regard iniquity in my heart, the Lord will not hear me."   Father, erase iniquity from my mind. May I see them through Your eyes? May I experience just a glimpse of the tender love You have for them? Fill me up, Lord. Let my cup of love overflow.

Father, I don't want anything to interrupt the communion I experience with You. Help me follow Jesus' example by expressing, "Father, forgive them for they know not what they are doing." Father, seal my lips-- just as the seraphim touched Isaiah's lips with the live coal from the fire to seal his lips, in your holy Word in Isaiah 6:6-7-- so that I won't share this hurt with anyone, but You, dear Father. Help me to be tenderhearted and forgiving, I pray, remembering the many times You, dear Father, have forgiven me.

Thank you, Father, in Jesus name, I pray.

With Love,

Gloria

James 3:15: For jealousy and selfishness are not God's kind of wisdom. Such things are earthly, unspiritual, inspired by the devil. For wherever there is jealousy or selfish ambition, there will be disorder and every other kind of evil. (CLB)

Jealousy

Dear Father,

Guard my heart against jealousy and selfishness. I realize where there is disorder there is confusion, and I know who is the author of confusion. You are the Author of peace and order (I Cor. 14:33). So if the twins, jealousy and selfishness, enter my thoughts send me an angel Lord, to usher them out of town. I'm on a mission for You, Lord, and I don't want anything to slow me down. I have a purpose that You have placed in my heart.

Show me places in my heart, Lord, that are still wounded so Your Word can apply the healing balm of Gilead that I need. Shine Your light on hurts that still linger from the past, Lord, because I know a wounded spirit can become selfish and self-centered. I don't want to waste time nursing old wounds, Lord, when You can heal them with the power of Your Word. I don't want my love to turn inward and dwell on myself. I want to be busy about Your business of loving others and exalting Your name to them. You are the Healer. I wait in Your

Guard my heart. Presence, oh Lord, Your blessed Presence, and expectantly await Your perfect healing. I bow before You Lord, admitting my dependence on You. I will wait for Your Power, I will wait for Your glory.

Father, guard my heart from Satan's traps. He's a master at getting Your children distracted. May I press on toward the goal and the prize of Jesus Christ. You are my Lord. In Jesus' name I pray.

With Love,

Gloria

John 1:1-2: In the beginning, (before all time) was the Word (Christ) and the Word was with God, and the Word was God, Himself. (2) He was present originally with God. (AMP)

Psalm 91:1: He who dwells in the secret place of the Most High shall remain stable and fixed under the shadow of the Almighty [Whose power no foe can withstand]. (AMP)

Jesus

Dear Lord,

Your grace is amazing and I reverence Your holiness. I sing triumphant praises to You, because You are the Victor. I sense Your very presence in the breath of the wind, the essence of You stirs my very soul.

You, dear Lord, represent love unspeakable. You dear Christ, took off Your royal garments and departed from being surrounded and engulfed with holiness to enter my world. You came for me. You came for my brothers and sisters. You are an awesome God and worthy, so worthy of my praise. The very light of You lights up my life. The Psalmist David expressed, "Create in me a pure heart and

"Create in me a pure heart." make my spirit right again. Do not send me away from You or take Your Holy Spirit away from me." Father, I surrender my heart to You. The Word tells us You will grant us the desires of our hearts, so Father I'm asking for a surrendered heart. I desire a willing heart that is conformed to You.

*F*ather, as I think of the sacrifice You made, I come to You with a humble, broken and contrite heart. I am so glad You are a merciful God. Change my heart, oh God, until it conforms to what You'd have it be. May I serve You all the days of my life. May I hide in the shadow of Your wings and have courage and Your strength when it's time to face the storm. I would be foolish, Lord, to expect earthly peace until You come for me. Your Word tells us in John 16:33, "These things I have spoken unto you, that in me ye might have peace. In the world ye shall have tribulation; but be of good cheer; I have overcome the world." So Father, I will claim and cherish peace in You, knowing my tribulation is in Your capable hands.

Thank you, dear Lord, for coming to earth and experiencing humanity. Thank You for becoming the Lamb of God. I could never express my gratitude enough to You. I pray for boldness and gentleness in sharing my heart and love for You with others. In Jesus' name I pray.

With Love,

Gloria

Isaiah 61:10: I will greatly rejoice in the Lord, my soul shall be joyful in my God for he hath clothed me with the garments of salvation, he hath covered me with the robe of righteousness, as a bridegroom decketh himself with ornaments, and as a bride adorneth herself with jewels. (KJV)

Revelation 19:8: And to her was granted that she should be arrayed in fine linen, clean and white; for the fine linen is the righteousness of saints. (KJV)

Savior

Dear Lord,

Thank You for Your dear, precious Son, Jesus. Jesus, for us, You gave up the splendor of Heaven, just for a while. The mission was too special, too significant to delegate. You came Yourself. You walked in our shoes; felt our pain of rejection; made choices, made friends, felt our losses. You were our

Deliverer, our Savior, and our one Hope for eternity. In all Your glory, Your precious, priceless blood had to be shed. As Your blood spilled from the cross of Calvary You breathed, "It is finished."

May I love You as no other. And You reached for my hand. As I reached for Your hand and felt it close over mine and felt the blood wash over me with forgiveness, I, too, was clothed in Your righteousness of fine, white linen. Thank You, precious Son of God, sweet Savior, for being my Deliverer, my Rescuer. I want to spend the rest of my days praising You, speaking of You, honoring You. May I love You as no other. May I see the brightness of Your glory to light my path until once again You leave the splendor of Heaven and come for me, in just a little while. In Jesus' name, I pray.

With Love,

Gloria

Psalms 34:7: The Angel of the Lord encamps around those who fear Him (who revere and worship Him with awe) and each of them He delivers. (AMP)

Psalms 145:20-21: The Lord preserves all those who love Him, but all the wicked will He destroy. My mouth shall speak the praise of the Lord; and let all flesh bless (affectionately and gratefully praise) His holy name forever and ever. (AMP)

Angel of The Lord

Dear Lord,

My heart's desire is to praise and worship You. May You send the angels of Heaven to teach me how to praise and worship. I want to make Psalm 145:5 "On the glorious splendor of Your majesty and on Your wondrous works I will meditate." (AMP), my heart's song. I praise You for being near to all Your children who call. I thank You for showering favor on me. May my lips speak of Your power and glory forever. May Psalm 18:1, be my soul's cry, "I love You fervently and devotedly, O Lord, my Strength." (AMP)

God, You are a protective Father. Psalm 18:6 tells me, "In my distress (when seemingly closed in) I called upon the Lord and cried to my God; He heard my voice out of His temple (heavenly dwelling place) and my cry came before Him, into His (very) ears. You tell me in Psalms 18:16 that You, great and mighty God, reached down from Heaven and took me and drew me out of my trials. You are the Deliverer.

Father, thank You for listening for my cries and thank You for listening for my praise and laughter. You, Father, are so worthy of praise. Help me love You more and sing praises and adoration to You all the days of eternity. In Jesus' name I pray.

With Love,

Gloria

II Samuel 22:11: (The Lord) was seen upon the wings of the wind.
Ephesians 3:19: And to know the love of Christ, which passeth knowledge, that ye might be filled with all the fullness of God. (KJV)

Beneath His Wings

Dear Lord,

How good it feels to be here, so strong and warm and secure beneath Your wings. Your love is all around me. I feel it on my left, on my right, all around me; even to the top of my head.

My heart is so full of Your love. I can barely wait to see You face to face. Help me to be a clean, pure vessel, empty and waiting to be filled with Your love. Your love is greater than anything I have ever known or could ever hope to know. I feel so unworthy and grateful at the same time.

51

*H*elp me, dear Father, to pass on that love and tell others about the great, powerful, all knowing, omnipresent, personal God You are. Help me to be a candle to someone's dark world. I want to spread the sunshine of Your mighty, powerful Word. I want to encourage and be strong for my brothers and sisters.

*P*lease grant me an overpowering love for Your children, for mankind, for the lost and needy. Change my heart, Oh, God, to be pleasing to You.

I'm your servant, Lord, and I feel so grateful and humble to even call myself Your servant. It still amazes me when I read in Your Holy Word, that You call us Your friend, for the servant doesn't know what the Master is doing but You, cherished Lord, share Your mission with us. I'm honored each time You entrust me with sharing Your precious, life-changing Word.

*O*h, how I adore You; I will praise Your holy, wonderful name forever. In Jesus' name I pray.

*W*ith *L*ove,

*G*loria

Ecclesiastes 3:11: God has given them a desire to know the future. He does everything just right and on time, but people can never completely understand what he is doing. (NCV)
Isaiah 55:8: The Lord says, "My thoughts are not like your thoughts. Your ways are not like my ways." (NCV)

God Is Never Tardy

Dear Lord,

Forgive me, Father sometimes I wonder where You are in my situation. Sometimes I forget that everything will be beautiful in Your time. I can't imagine having the mind of Christ, even though I know from Your Word that this is what I'm to strive for.

Jesus, the Word tells me You were here and felt every temptation that was known to man. Did You ever feel the task too great, the mission too impossible? Did You ever feel like throwing in the towel? But we know the rest of the story: You just kept pressing on.

*S*ome days, Father, it's so easy to stay focused on You and Your holiness and it's so easy to pray without ceasing. It's so easy to pass every thought and desire by You first. Then there are days when I come crashing down to earth fully realizing that I live here, and so many situations seem chronic and out of my control. That's when I lift my eyes toward heaven and cry out, "God are You still there? Did You see what just happened? Did You hear what was said? When, God, when? When are You going to move in this situation?"

Help me to study Your Word.

*F*orgive me, Father; help me to study Your Word and know that You and You alone are God. Help me to realize that You are never tardy, and that my best interest is always on Your mind. Father, may I be a blessing to someone else today and not think about my situations. Help me to think of others first.

I love You, Father, and place my cares on You. In Jesus' name I pray.

With *L*ove,

*G*loria

54

John 14:26: But the Comforter which is the Holy Ghost, whom the Father will send in my name, He shall teach you all things, and bring all things to your remembrance, whatsoever I have said unto you. (KJV)

The Comforter

Dear Lord,

Help me to remember Father, when the hour seems the darkest, that You left the Comforter with us. When the valleys seem the deepest and the dark shadows plunge me into the deepest despair, I don't have to abide there. Help me to remember Your Word. Help me to feel the intimacy of Your nearness. Help my weary soul sing a love song back to You.

Thank you Father, for the reassurance that I'm never alone. No valley too deep, no place too

dark, but the Comforter is there. Thank You for
Your Word and Your mighty promises that are ever
present from generation to generation. I
know Father, that You are eternity.
Praise Your name! With gratitude I sing,
that I have Your Presence even in the
darkest moments of my life. You are a
gracious, loving Father. I praise You for
Your thoughtfulness. I praise You for Your
protection. But most of all, I praise You because
You said, in Proverbs 8:17 (KJV), "I love them that
love Me; and those that seek me early shall find
Me." In Jesus' name I pray.

" I love them that love Me."

With Love,

Gloria

Psalm 91:1-2,4: He that dwelleth in the secret place of the most High shall abide under the shadow of the Almighty. I will say of the Lord He is my refuge and my fortress; my God; in Him will I trust. (4) He shall cover thee with his feathers, and under His wings shalt thou trust. (KJV)

The Secret Place

Dear Lord,

El Shaddai (more than enough), I come to You with love in my heart. I want to abide under Your shadow. I want to run and find shelter under Your wings. Take me, Father, to that secret place of the most High. I know that in Your presence I find peace, joy, and love unspeakable. It feels so warm and secure here. I never want to leave Your protection. I want You, Lord, the most high, to be my habitation. Abba, thank You for giving the angels charge over me, to keep and protect me. (Psalms 91:11) All glory to You, God. All honor belongs to You. I'll never forget what You have done for me. You and You alone are worthy of my praise. My heart writes love songs to You. All the days of my life I want to serve You and sing Your praises.

My heart writes love songs to You.

You are My Helper. You tell me in Psalm 91:15 that I may call upon You and You WILL ANSWER. You will be with me in trouble and You WILL DELIVER and honor me. Help me be as faithful to You. When I hear Your voice, help me respond quickly, "Yes, Lord." You are the one I adore. Thank You for Your loving kindness every morning. You are Righteousness. In Jesus' Name, I pray.

With Love,

Gloria

1 Corinthians 15:52-53: In a moment, in the twinkling of an eye, at the last trump: for the trumpet shall sound, and the dead shall be raised incorruptible, and we shall be changed. For this corruptible must put on incorruption, and this mortal must put on immortality. (KJV)

Gabriel's Trumpet

Dear Lord,

Thank You for holding me today. For some reason, Lord, I'm lonesome to hear Gabriel's trumpet. I can see the bright streets of gold now. Some day soon, I'll behold Your lovely face. Today, Father, my eyes strain as I look toward the eastern sky. I long to see Your face.

Father, I know my earthly life is comprised of mountains and valleys. You have taught me well that I can't live on the mountain. Remember when all my friends told me, "Gloria you just can't camp on the mountain?" That night, I prayed "Father, let me

59

stay just a little longer." And dear Father, I felt the light of Your smile as You allowed me to stay on the mountain and just bask in Your light and Your love just a little bit longer. I know so well, Father, that I don't grow on the mountain; growth takes place in the valley. Dear, beloved Father, I don't want to stay a baby and feast on milk. I want to grow in Your wisdom and strength. I desire my mind to feed on eternal things. I want to listen with my soul instead of my ears. I wish to speak with my heart instead of my lips. I want to love not with my mind but through the Holy Spirit who lives within.

I'm beginning to understand, Father. The more I focus my attention, my life, my mind, my heart on You, it doesn't matter if I'm on the mountain or in the valley, because You never, ever leave me. Teach me, Father, to die to self and let You live through me.

You are a holy, gracious, precious, personal God and I love You. I just want to be where You are. I want to experience Your Presence all the days of my life. In Jesus' name, I pray.

With Love,

Gloria

Ephesians 2:8: For it is by free grace (God's unmerited favor) that you are saved (delivered from judgment and made partakers of Christ's salvation) through (your) faith. And this (salvation) is not of yourselves (of your own doing, it came not through your own striving), but it is the gift of God. (AMP)

God's Unmerited Favor

Dear Lord,

It seems that no matter how much my heart dwells on you and I bask in your love, I still wander away. It's as if I'm in a forest and concentrating only on you. I'm on a winding path. Sometimes it gets so dim I can barely see the path, but there is a song in my heart. When I stop to make a decision on which way to go, I hear the still, small voice humming in my heart, "Go to your left", or "No, this time take a right."

Sometimes I see flowers in the distance and I wander off the path to smell the fragrance that entices me. The diversion that takes me off my path is sometimes as innocent as a deer swiftly running by and I run to catch up with it. Regardless of what distracts me, I suddenly look up and I'm off track. I'm off the trail and I've lost my way.

Praise you, Jesus, that You left Your throne and came searching for me. If You hadn't, I would have been lost forever. You gave me *You came looking for me.* salvation as a gift. You knew I wouldn't be able to earn it. You knew I would get distracted. You knew I wouldn't make the trip. No matter how clear You made the instructions, You knew I'd wander so far off the trail that sometimes, even though I knew Your voice was there, I wouldn't be able to understand what You were saying. I'd be too far away, caught up in the flowers or the deer playing.

So dear, precious, loving Savior, You couldn't bear for me to be lost forever. You dropped Your robe and gave up your crown to plunge head first into my world. You came looking for me.

It was nothing I did. It was Your gift to me. You even took the judgment against me and stood in my place. You didn't make a wrong decision, I did. But You loved me so much, You took my punishment.

Father, as long as I live, I'll never quit being amazed at Your grace. I'm amazed as I read that I am Your handiwork, Your workmanship, Your master-piece. I feel so ordinary but Your word tells me otherwise.

Father, grant me opportunities to share this great truth with others. Father give me the desire to STOP on this journey of life and share how very much You love us, that it was You who delivered us. All I have to do is look at You with the eyes of a child; eyes that trust, and have faith to believe in Your free grace and partake of Your Salvation.

I am Your handi-work.

Father, my heart, soul and spirit are bound to You, not by the law, but by love. I love You, Father. In Jesus' name I pray.

With Love,

Gloria

James 1:25:   But the truly happy people are those who carefully study God's perfect law that makes people free, and they continue to study it. They do not forget what they heard, but they obey what God's teaching says. Those who do this will be made happy. (NCV)

Happiness

Dear Father,

The little word "obey" is such a profound one. There are so many distractions in this life striving for our attention.   Father, here we are right in the middle of the information age. We are flooded, actually saturated with information; more facts on every topic imaginable. Some days are so draining just trying to decide what data I am going to absorb.   Father, keep me focused on You.   Help me to find my strength and refuge in You.   I know Your Word holds truth and

Your Word paves my way to happiness. Help me to rest in You.

Father, the world shouts its definition of happiness and Your Word whispers truths, unfolds **Turn** secrets, and defines my life into **my** eternity. Father, I ask You to close **heart** my mind to anything that gets in the **and** **eyes** way of You. Father, tilt my chin **on** toward You, lift my eyes to lock gaze **You.** with You, turn my inquisitive mind towards Your truth. Help me wear truth as a warm blanket. Give me the spirit of obedience. I present to You my will. Please turn my heart and eyes on You. Thank you, Father, for the song in my heart and the great expectation I have of Your making and molding my life. In Jesus' name I pray.

With Love,

Gloria

James 3:17: But the wisdom that comes from heaven is first of all pure and full of quiet gentleness. Then it is peace-loving and courteous. It allows discussion and is willing to yield to others; it is full of mercy and good deeds. It is wholehearted and straightforward and sincere. (CLB)

Peace In My Heart

Dear Lord,

Holy Messiah, King of Kings, that holy gift I pursue is wisdom. From Your holy, inspired Word, I've learned that wisdom holds the key to success. I know success is peace of mind, love, honor, but most of all, wisdom is being in Your presence, as wisdom can come only from You dear Father. While in Your presence may I bask in Your purity, in Your love, in Your righteousness, as peace like a river floods my soul.

Father, may this passionate pursuit for wisdom never dim. Your wisdom is undefiled and pure. You tell me your wisdom is full of gentleness; it is courteous, willing to yield to others, and full of mercy. Your wisdom is straightforward and sincere. With wisdom, my harvest will be full of peace and goodness.

Father, lead me. As I am surrounded by Your presence, let Your light shine on the recesses of my soul. May I learn to pursue only things that are pure, things that are righteous, things that will last into eternity.

Father, You and You alone are the one and only true God. I desire Your presence for the rest of my days. In Jesus' name, I pray.

With Love,

*G*loria

Psalm 16:7: I will bless the Lord who counsels me; he gives me wisdom in the night. He tells me what to do. (TLB)

Wisdom In The Night

Dear Lord,

So many times I have received Your wise counsel at night. It seems at night babies' fevers go higher; problems look like giants in the shadows of twilight. You come to me with wise counsel at my greatest need and bring me wisdom. You, dear Father, tell me what to do. I read in Psalm 18:18 (TLB), "On the day when I was weakest, they attacked. But the Lord held me steady. (19) He led me to a place of safety, for He delights in me. (20) The Lord rewarded me for doing right and being pure." Father, let's stop right there.

Let me ponder this for a minute. How can I, a mere mortal, be pure? How do I do that?

 $\mathcal{P}$ salm 11:4 (TLB), "But the Lord is still in His holy temple; He still rules from heaven. He closely watches everything that happens here on earth." Thank You Lord, for reminding me that You closely watch me, but again, Father, I ask, how can I be pure? I know, not by my own strength, but by the blood of Jesus, and the Holy Spirit living in my temple, and by faith. But Father, what do You mean by "pure?" Psalm 15:3 (TLB), "Anyone who refuses to slander others, does not listen to gossip, never harms his neighbor, speaks out against sin, criticizes those committing it, commends the faithful followers of the Lord, keeps a promise even if it ruins him, does not crush his debtors with high interest rates, and refuses to testify against the innocent despite bribes offered him - such a man (woman) will stand firm forever."

"I keep the Lord before me always."

 $\mathcal{F}$ ather, I make Your words mine and sing back to You, Psalm 16:7 (NCV), "I praise the Lord because He advises me, even at night, I feel His leading. (8) I keep the Lord before me always, because He is close by my side, I will not be hurt. (11) YOU WILL TEACH ME TO LIVE A HOLY LIFE. Being with You will fill me with joy; at Your right hand I will find pleasure forever." Wow what can I say? You are the great Raboni teacher.

In Psalm 14:5 (TLB) "... God is with those who love Him."

Teach me, Raboni, to love You more. In Jesus' name I pray.

With Love,

Gloria

II Timothy 1:6-7: That is why I would remind you to stir up (rekindle the embers of, fan the flame of, and keep burning) the (gracious) gift of God, (the inner fire) that is in you by means of the laying on of my hands (with those of the elders at your ordinance. For God did not give us a spirit of timidity (of cowardice, of craven and cringing and fawning fear) but (He has given us a spirit) of power and of love and of calm and well-balanced mind and discipline and self-control. (AMP)

A Sound Mind

Dear Lord

Protect my mind, dear Father. The more I saturate my soul and mind with Your Word the more perverted some of the world's entertainment seems. Guard my mind dear Father, so that it focuses on truth and Your glory. Do not permit me to be deceived. I pray for my family to have great and mighty wisdom on what they will allow to penetrate their minds. I pray with great travail that You will protect them from the deceiver who will cause their senses to become deadened and numb to the Devil's lies. Keep our minds sharp and alert and wise to the deceptive measures of our enemy. Open our eyes Lord, and open our ears. Allow us to see and hear with Your eyes and Your ears. Grant us discernment, Lord.

Father, we thank You for the fire of the Holy Spirit You left to live in us when we became children of God. Grant us a desire to read and meditate on Your Word so we can fan the flame that took up residence within our spirit when we first asked You into our hearts. Help us to be bold and share Your precious Son's name with all we meet. May Your name slip easily from our lips, our cherished Redeemer, as we tell others of Your mighty power and glory.

Protect my family, Lord. Draw them to You. You are my Lord. In Jesus' name I pray.

With Love,

Gloria

Psalms 141:2: Let my prayer be set forth before thee as incense; and the lifting up of my hands as the evening sacrifice. (KJV)

Fragrance Of Adoration

Dear Lord,

Oh, how I desire to be a sweet fragrance to You. Let my praise of adoration enter the throne room as a loving daughter. May I dwell in Your presence forever. May my thoughts of love reach Your heart and the incense of my love linger with You.

I can still hardly believe that You loved me before I even acknowledged who You were. I can still see You reaching out to me with Your loving care and I repaid You with rejection. I spent so much time dreaming instead of meditating. Dreaming what I would become someday when I grew up. I spent hours on what my house would look like, how wonderful the man I married would be, how many children I wanted, and what my contribution to this world would be. But I forgot You, dear Father.

I fell in love with my Creator I left You out. I left You out not for a little while but for most of my life. Dear Father, forgive me. I was so busy trying to be good, doing the right thing, as I saw it, that I forgot to look up. I forgot to build a relationship with You. I forgot the most important thing. But You dear Father, never gave up on me. You kept reaching. You kept calling. I'm eternally grateful that You did. And one glorious day, I looked up and I fell in love with my Creator. I acknowledged perfect love, perfect acceptance and oh, the joy that flooded my soul. Dear Father, I will never be the same. You are my reason for being.

Father, I lift my hands in praise and love to You. Let my prayer be a sweet fragrance to You as You read the melody in my heart that is full of love; love for my Creator. In Jesus' name I pray.

With Love,

Gloria

Isaiah 40:11: He will feed His flock like a shepherd; He will gather the lambs in His arm, He will carry them in His bosom and will gently lead those that have their young. (AMP)

Jennifer

Dear Lord,

As I read the above scripture, my daughter-in-law came to mind. I praise You dear Jesus for granting my heart's desire that day I breathed the prayer, "Father, may I see her through Your eyes?" The beauty, I beheld! I still feel a tingle and my heart moves with compassion. I experienced just a glimpse of the love You have for her. Tears filled my eyes as I too experienced some of that love entering into my spirit. My God, You are more than any words I could possibly put to pen. You take my breath away.

I'm so glad You have Jennifer in Your arms and close to Your bosom. Feed her well dear Father. I'm so glad You took time in Your Holy Word to assure us that You will gently lead those that have their young. Take care of her, Father with tenderness, and draw her unto You. Give her strength as she devotedly cares for the twin babies You blessed her and my son with. Tuck her in at night as she closes her eyes for a well- deserved rest after a long day. Send angels to soothe her brow as she sleeps and while resting looks like a child herself.

Make her wise in Your word.

*T*hank You Father, for entrusting her to us. Make her wise in Your Word, Father, so she'll have wisdom to pass on to her children. Each and every day help her to love You more. Accomplish the purpose You designed just for her as You hovered over her in her mother's womb.

*M*ay Your Presence and love linger over their household and it truly be a home that lives and loves Jesus. In Jesus' name I pray.

With *L*ove,

*G*loria

Psalm 56:8: You number and record my wanderings; put my tears into Your bottle - are they not in Your book? (AMP) You have seen me tossing and turning through the night. You have collected all my tears and preserved them in your bottle! You have recorded every one in your book. (TLB)

Tears In A Bottle

Dear Lord,

What a tender, loving Father you are. You are Abba, You are the King. You are the Creator, even so, You are the tender Father, the Father, who watches Your children as we sleep. Your Holy Word has such clarity. You are a tender Father who takes time to see each tear that falls but more than that, a tender Father who catches each tear and preserves it in a bottle. Your name is Love; a love that is so deep I can't fathom it.

79

Father, You certainly do lead by example. Please plant that seed of love deep in my heart. Water it with Your Word. You tell us dear Father, in Psalm 11, that you watch closely everything that happens here on earth, as You sit on your throne in heaven. Help us pass Your tests. We know from as early as elementary school that we can't go to the next level until we pass the test. As you test us Father, help us search for Your goodness, help us be doers not just hearers of the Word. Help us receive promotion so that we may go on to the next level You intend for us. Protect us, Father, from the evil one. Cover our households with Your blessed wings of protection. You've compared yourself to the hen that covers her young with her wings of protection (Matt.37). May we gather in under Your wings.

Protect us Father from the evil one.

Father, in Psalm 11, You continue to tell us that the godly shall see Your face. Help us Father, to be Godly and righteous through the power of Your Son, Jesus. Help us to rest in Your lavish love.

Keep me, Father, in the shadow of Your wings as I continue on my journey in search of truth, honor and serving You.

Keep my foot from slipping Father. Father, I long to see Your face, but for now, I'll stay in the shadow of Your wings and feel You hovering. There is no place like Your Presence and basking in Your love.

Thanks for drying my tears. In the sweet name of Jesus I pray.

With Love,

Gloria

Psalm 127:2: ...for He gives (blessings) to His beloved in sleep. (AMP)

Isaiah 49:16: Behold, I have indelibly imprinted (tattooed a picture of) you on the palm of each of My hands; (O Zion) your walls are continually before me. (AMP)

On The Palm of His Hand

Dear Lord,

I used to share with my three sons how You waited with great anticipation for the hour they would awaken so You could talk with them. One time I was sharing with them about how excited You were to hear from them. You gazed on them while they slept, just waiting for them to wake up and visit with You. My little son, with big blue eyes, exclaimed while shaking his head no, "Uh-huh Mommy, He didn't wait until I was awake, He talked to me while I was sleeping." How special, how wonderful, that the omnipresent God, would love us enough to want to be involved in every aspect of our lives. Father, I'm so glad, so very glad, that I'll have eternity to spend in Your presence.

Father, thank you for blessing me with three of the most wonderful sons in the world. I am blessed. When they smile, my heart fills up with love. You understand Father; You have The Son. Thank You for giving them to me to share love with.

Only You, Father, with Your everlasting love, would think of engraving our names on the palm of Your hand. I'm so glad I am Your child. I feel so safe and secure in the palm of Your hand. I cherish You, dear Father. Please continue to renew my mind, even as I sleep. In the name of Jesus, I pray.

With Love,

Gloria

Jeremiah 17:9: The heart is deceitful above all things and desperately wicked: who can know it? (KJV)

Deceitful Heart

Dear Lord,

I grew up on fairy tales and the yellow brick road. It sounded so warm and right, to respond to life with "just trust your heart." It all sounded so "warm and fuzzy."

Father, help me to understand that sin is not a product of my circumstances or my performance, it is a product of my heart. Change my heart, oh, Lord. Make it acceptable to You. Give me a new heart that is pursuing You and Your ways. Please strengthen my heart, so I may be committed to You. Help me Father, to love You with all my heart.

You have told us in Psalm 8:5 that You have made man a little lower than the angels and have crowned him with glory and honor. So when my heart tells me I'm all alone it tries to deceive me, because a God who knew me in my mother's womb, (Isaiah 44:2), numbered the hairs on my head

God will never leave or forsake me. (Matthew 10:30) and sings over me (Zephaniah 3:17) could never abandon me. A Father, who writes stories in His Word-- like the beloved story of the prodigal son-- for me to obtain wisdom and guidance, has to be a God who will never leave or forsake me. You sacrificed Your only Son, so I could have life eternally. Oh, what a loving Father You are. How can I ever express my loving gratitude to You? I will shout from the rooftops your great love, El Shaddai, (caregiver). In Jesus' name, I pray.

With Love,

Gloria

Romans 8:3-5: The law was without power, because the law was made weak by our sinful selves. But God did what the law could not do. He sent his own Son to earth with the same human life that others use for sin. By sending his Son to be an offering to pay for sin, God used a human life to destroy sin. He did this so that we could be the kind of people the law correctly wants us to be. Now we do not live following our sinful selves, but we live following the Spirit. (NCV)

Grace

Dear Savior,

Words cannot express the feelings I am having at this moment. As I read Paul's words in Romans, I saw faith and grace as never before. Father, a new revelation raced through my mind as I saw Your love sprinkled all over these pages. I saw the God, an Abba Father, who tells us in Isaiah 30:18 (NAS), "Therefore the Lord longs to be gracious to you...how blessed are those who long for Him." It comforts me to hear You say in Your Word, "I have called you by name; you are mine." (Isaiah 43:1) Father my heart overflows, when You tell me, "...I will pour out My Spirit on your offspring." Isaiah 44:3-4 (NAS), the God who tells me to love my neighbor as myself, a Father who *You did it all for Your beloved children.* can't stand to see His children go to Hell. The Father who sacrificed His only begotten, perfect Son, so I, too, would have a chance to live with Him throughout eternity. You knew, Father, that I wouldn't be able to keep the law; You knew I would stumble. With Your boundless love, You did it all for your beloved children. You tell us to hide Your Word in our hearts. It's in my heart and in my mouth. Your Word says all I have to do is believe and confess with my mouth," Jesus is Lord", and indeed He is. He is my Lord, my Savior and I believe in my heart that You Father, raised Him from the dead. A thousand times over, I believe Your Word says I will be saved. We believe in our hearts and are made right with You and confess with our lips. (Rom.10:8-10).

You are the very essence of Grace and Mercy; such love. And if that weren't enough, You left us the Holy Spirit to live within us to comfort us, to guide us, to even pray for us when we are too weak or do not know how to pray for ourselves. You, great God, allowed us to be grafted into the olive tree. You allowed us to become your adopted sons and daughters.

Father, please continue to renew my mind. Increase my faith, Father, help me want to be a living sacrifice to You. Father, draw me to the Holy Spirit, help me to listen so that I will be pleasing to You. Continually remind me to defeat evil by doing good.

Increase my faith.

Father, I can't comprehend the magnitude of Your love, grace and mercy, but I receive it with joy and humbleness. Direct me, Father; show me where You desire me to go. My life is in Your hands, and I'm so glad it is.

Jesus, sweet name of Jesus, thank You for being obedient and loving us as the Father loved You. You are an awesome God. May I have a hunger to tell others of Your greatness, Your gentleness, Your sacrifice, Your redeeming power, but most of all about Your love. In Jesus' name I pray.

With Love,

Gloria

Lamentations 3:22-23: It is of the Lord's mercies that we are not consumed because his compassions fail not. They are new every morning: great is thy faithfulness. (KJV)

New Every Morning

Dear Lord,

You Father, are new every morning to me. And, Father, You are all things to me. You are a God of many facets. If I live a thousand years, I would not be finished discovering all Your traits. As I discover in Your Holy Word there are many names for You. I call You Father, I call You Abba (Daddy), I call You Love, I call You Mercy, I call You Joy, I call You Truth, I call You Provider, I call You Friend, I call You Jesus, I call You Holy Spirit, I call You Lord, I call You Grace, I call You Holy, I call You High Priest, I call You

Restorer, I call You Wisdom, I call You King of Glory. Mercy and grace are like twin magnets that draw me to you. Without them I couldn't enter Your presence. Humbly, I bow before You, thanking You for making a provision for me to enter Your presence. Father, You are addictive. The more time I spend with You the more time I want with You. I've learned to bask in Your love. I love to linger in Your holiness. Thank You for washing me in the blood and giving me white crisp linen to wear. (Rev. 19:8)

Hold me in the palm of Your hand, Father. In Jesus' name I pray.

With Love,

Gloria

Luke 19:37-40 "As He (Jesus) was approaching (the city) at the descent of the Mount Olives, the whole crowd of the disciples began to rejoice and to praise God (extolling Him exultantly and) loudly for all the mighty miracles and works of power that they had witnessed. Crying, Blessed (celebrated with praises) is the King Who comes in the name of the Lord! Peace in heaven (freedom there from all the distresses that that are experienced as the result of sin) and glory (majesty and splendor) in the highest (heaven). And Some of the Pharisees from the throng said to Jesus, Teacher, reprove Your disciples! (4) He (Jesus) replied, I tell you that if these keep silent, the very stones will cry out." (AMP)

Stones Will Cry Out

Dear Lord,

Oh, Father, I desire that we may be known as a generation that praises You. I've spent so many years being Your child but ignoring You. I wonder how many times the stones cried out as I forgot to thank You, I forgot to bask in Your love; I forgot to interact with You, I forgot to focus on Your beauty and delight in You; I forgot to be still and let You teach me.

*F*orgive me Father, as I forgot to rejoice in the very nature of who You are.

*M*ay praise and joy fill my heart as I exalt You for the power, love, authority, and tender care You have displayed in my life.

*M*ay my home ring out in praise and adoration in unison with all of creation as we and the angels worship and adore You. In Jesus' name I pray.

*W*ith *L*ove,

*G*loria

Luke 18:16: But Jesus called them unto him, and said, "Suffer little children to come unto me, and forbid them not for of such is the Kingdom of God." (KJV)

Isaiah 42:6: The Lord says, "I, the Lord, called you to do right, and I will hold your hand and protect you." (NCV)

Help Me Do What Is Right

Dear Lord,

I heard a little boy pray today. He prayed only one sentence. He said, "Father, help me do what is right." It was the most powerful, sincere prayer, I think I've ever heard. Thank you, Father, for allowing me to experience this moment in his life. Thank you for honoring me by allowing me to be right there as he bowed his head. Such wisdom for a boy ten years old! I could hear the crash of your mighty ocean in the background and the seagulls calling out. I could smell the freshness of a new day, a new beginning. But nothing could compare as time stood still for a little boy to pray. The ocean lost its splendor. The sea gulls became silent, I could hear the shush of nature. After all, a child of the King bowed his head to pray. I could feel Your presence so strong.

A child of the King bowed his head.

Father, help me to be as sincere as that little boy was. Help me to experience Your mercy and grace. Help me to whisper a prayer of expectation as I kneel and say, "Help me Lord, do what is right."

Father, You never stop amazing me. Today You used a child, a little boy, to point me in the right direction. Thank you for allowing me to experience Your gaze on a little boy. I know your heart was so blessed and pleased. You are a gracious, Holy God and I adore You. In Jesus' name I pray.

With Love,

Gloria

Jeremiah 31:16: Thus saith the Lord; Refrain thy voice from weeping, and thine eyes from tears; for thy work shall be rewarded, saith the Lord; and they shall come again from the land of the enemy. (KJV)

Matthew 5:44: But I say unto you, Love your enemies, bless them that curse you, do good to them that hate you, and pray for them which despitefully use you, and persecute you. (KJV)
Philippians 2:7: but made himself of no reputation, and took upon him the form of a servant, and was made in the likeness of men. (KJV)

Refrain From Weeping

Dear Lord,

You are a tender, loving, soothing, comforting Father. I remember so well arising very early one morning a long time ago. My sleep was troubled. I was restless. I tossed and turned. I was angry. I was hurt. In my heart I kept crying out to you, "Father, this isn't fair." I could hear you speaking in my spirit, saying, "My precious child, it rains on the just and the unjust." "But Father", I cried out, "What about my reputation?" You replied, "I made myself of no reputation." I just couldn't be soothed. I continued crying out, "Father, this is so unfair. I'm not guilty." You, my precious Abba replied, "Neither was I, my child." I remember so well just collapsing in a chair while I held my head in my hands, tears running down my face, crying, "I can't stand this Father, help me." I picked up my Bible, and breathed, "Speak to me, Abba. I must hear from You. I must find comfort."

*I*mmediately, you heard my cry and it was no accident that as I opened my Bible it fell open to Jeremiah 31:16. My eyes fell on that particular verse and all other verses seemed to fade away. Father, you spoke so tenderly through Your Word to me. It was so soothing to my soul that I could feel Your presence close to me. It was as if You were reading the scripture to me. Your Words penetrated my soul and I have not forgotten them to this day. I remember well, feeling the word "forgive" vibrate through my soul. I knew I had to, and You had told me to refrain from weeping, but I

I could feel Your presence close to me.

still had to ask You how. Father, it just didn't seem natural to forgive. How do I forgive?

*T*hank You beloved Father, that You sent Your special pastor with such words of wisdom to me. I wrote every word on my heart. I still remember it as if it were yesterday. He said, "Gloria, you've been wounded. The wound is deep and the gash is gapping. If you allow any dirt to get in this wound it will fester and cause you pain forever. The scar will be ugly. If *Where I am weak You are strong.* you choose to keep it clean and not allow any dirt to get in, it will heal so clean that years from now the scar will be almost invisible. The choice is yours." I knew in my strength I could not do this. I knew that where I am weak You are strong. I knew I must cry out, "Father, rescue me. Only through Your living in me can this be possible. I want to forgive but I can't on my own. I hand it all to You, to use Your supernatural power to transform me." Immediately, I felt my heart soften and You, my precious Father gave me my heart's desires, and oh, the beauty I beheld. At last I was free indeed.

*F*ather, thank You for teaching me to forgive; now once again, I ask You to bless my enemies by drawing them closer to You.

Father, as I continue to walk forgiving and being forgiven, help me to keep my eyes on You. I learned that the definition of freedom is forgiving and being forgiven. Without you, I'd surely fall, and I don't want to spend one moment separated from You and I know unforgiveness, Father, will separate me from You. Teach me your ways, my Abba Father. I know Your Word tells us, You have plans to prosper us, not harm us. Help me stay focused on You and Your Word. Hold me in the palm of Your hand.

With Love,

Gloria

Matthew 8:17: He did those things to bring about what Isaiah the prophet had said: "He took our suffering on him and carried our diseases." (NCV)

Isaiah 53:4: But he took our suffering on him and felt our pain for us. We saw his suffering and thought God was punishing him. 5. "But he was wounded for the wrong we did; he was crushed for the evil we did. The punishment, which made us well, was given to Him, and we are healed because of His wounds. (NCV)

Jehovah - Rapha
God, My Healer

Dear Jehovah-Rapha,

You are my God. You are so faithful to me. I know Father, You are the Great Healer. Sometimes the illness we pray to You about is not visible to others. It can be a broken heart or old emotional wounds that have not healed properly. Father, my prayer, Jehovah-Rapha, is that You will create in us a whole and healthy body as we go about Your business. We praise You and thank You that because of Your wounds, we are set free and healed.

My God, may I turn loose of old hurts and broken hearts and let You, the great Healer, overshadow me with Your healing power. Wherever Your presence lingers, healing occurs. The power of Calvary sets the captive free. May I trust You, always, with any illness that befalls me. You are Raboni, Teacher, the greatest Teacher to ever live. Teach us, Father to exercise our faith and believe that You and only You are the great Physician.

The greatest Teacher to ever live.

Father, God, You are our Healer. May we be faithful to pray and receive what You have already done for us two thousand years ago. You, dear Savior, paid for our healing. May we praise and honor You for Your faithfulness to heal and trust You to do what is best. I know You are ABLE, and I trust You to do what is best for me. In Jesus' name I pray.

With Love,

Gloria

2 Corinthians 5:17-18: If anyone belongs to Christ, there is a new creation. The old things have gone; everything is made new! All this is from God. Through Christ, God made peace between us and himself, and God gave us the work of telling everyone about the peace we can have with him. (NCV)

Jehovah-Shalom God, My Peace

Dear Jehovah-Shalom,

The God of Peace. We know, Father, that by drinking in the living water we will find Your peace. Father, please rain Your word on me. That is where I will find life anew. I seek after Your peace that passes all understanding. I want to abide there, not just visit from time to time. I want to make Your peace my dwelling place. I know that with worship and praise I may enter into Your peace, knowing You can carry me above the storms in my life.

Lord, I need a fresh touch, a glowing encounter with You. I remember when I first gave my heart to You; I was tirelessly telling everyone I met about this great plan of salvation. The name of Jesus slipped so easily from my lips. I found I just couldn't love You without loving Your children. I wanted everyone I met to be introduced to Your love and protection. Please renew my heart, soul and mind. Give me a passion to tell others of Your great peace once again.

Thank You, Father, for being Jehovah-Shalom, our mighty God of Peace. We know with Your peace we will have victory over our enemies. Thank you for the peace that flows in and out of my heart like a river.

You, great King, are a mighty God and I praise You. In Jesus' name I pray.

With Love,

Gloria

Genesis 22:13-14: Abraham looked up and there in a thicket he saw a ram caught by its horn. He went over and took the ram and sacrificed it as a burnt offering instead of his son. So Abraham called that place The Lord Will Provide. (NIV)

John 3:16: God so loved the World that He offered in sacrifice His one and only Son, whom he loves. (NIV)

Jehovah-Jireh
God, My Provider

Dear Jehovah-Jireh,

The first time we saw the word love was in Genesis when You, dear Father, told Abraham to take his son, "whom thou lovest" and offer him there. But when the final hour came, You dear Father, were faithful and compassionate and provided the sacrifice by providing the ram. And when we couldn't follow the law and the rules, You once again rescued us but this time with the greatest expression of love the world has ever known or will ever know. You provided the sacrifice of Your perfect, precious Son. You are the God that provides. The extent of Your love is overwhelming and incomprehensible. I bow before You Lord, with my feeble expressions of Love, to a God who knew I'd stumble before I was aware of it. How I praise and adore You. Help me to open my heart and receive that love to its fullest so I may pass on this love to others. You are the great I Am and nothing is too big for my God. Your word tells us You are never tardy.   You'll always be on time.   We can depend on You.   Our waiting increases our faith as we wait for Your manifestation.

I'm so grateful that You, dear Lord, are the great Provider. In Jesus' name I pray.

With Love,

Gloria

Psalm 23:1-4:   The Lord is my shepherd, I shall not want, I have everything I need. He lets me rest in green pastures. He leads me to calm water. He gives me new strength. He leads me on the paths that are right for the good of His name. Even if I walk through a very dark valley, I will not be afraid, because you are with me. (NCV)

Jehovah - Rohi
God, My Shepherd

Dear Jehovah-Rohi,

You are my Shepherd and my Strength. Father, I love the story of the shepherd who had 100 sheep, lost one and left the 99 to look for the one. How many times have I been that one that left the flock? Your mercy and grace never fail to amaze me. I honor and thank You that You always draw me back. The power of Your Word is a mighty force that attracts like a magnet. My prayer is that I will remain faithful to You and not take my eyes from You. I pray that You will continue to draw me to Your Word. Without Your Word I would become perplexed and detached from You. You breathed the Word and I know that is how You commune with us. I want to rush with great expectation each day for Your Word. May I learn to pray without ceasing, to stay in Your presence, and meditate on Your Word.

You breathed the Word.

Father, send me out each day with wisdom and strength straight from Your majestic heart. I want more than anything to be a blessing and a light. Help me when I sin, to quickly confess and repent. Help me to pull in so close to You and spend so much time with You that I start to talk like You, walk like You, and make decisions like You, but most of all Father, help me learn to love like You.

Thank You, dear Shepherd, and may I have a pure heart. In Jesus' name I pray.

With Love,

Gloria

What's Love? Just Whisper Jesus

There were two young women living in the same house. Both were unmarried and expecting a child. One young woman gave birth and three days later the other woman gave birth. Both young women slept with their babies. One night one of the women rolled over in her sleep on her baby and smothered it. When she realized the dreadful thing that had happened, *She removed the other woman's son.* she slipped into the other young woman's room, with her dead child. She removed the other woman's son from her sleeping arms and replaced her healthy, very much alive son with the dead baby. The next morning when the young woman awoke and tried to feed her son, she realized the precious baby was dead. When daylight broke and the mother could see, she realized that this was not even her baby and that she had been tricked.

A very emotional argument broke out and both women decided to let the king settle the argument. Both appeared before King Solomon. The young women began telling their story, excitedly interrupting each other. They argued back and forth before the king.

The king tried to gather the facts so he could make a decision on who the baby belonged to. He asked for a sword to be brought to him. He explained to both that he was going to divide the living child in two and give half to each of them. At once, the real mother cried out to the king, "Stop, don't kill my son; give him to her, just don't kill him." But the other young woman agreed with the King, saying, "All right, divide the son between us, then it will be neither mine nor hers."

He asked for a sword to be brought to him.

Then the king ruled by saying, "Hand the baby to the woman who wants the child to live, for this is the real mother." I Kings 3:17-28 (CLB).

Webster's dictionary describes love as, "A profoundly tender, passionately affection for another person, or an intense personal attachment or affection, or strong enthusiasm or liking." It's still missing something isn't it? Let's explore a little more. Let's see what God says about love. The first evidence I see of love demonstrated toward man was when God said, "Let us (Father, Son and Holy Spirit) make mankind in Our image, after Our likeness..." Gen.1:26. (AMP). Wow, in His Holy Image.

How much He must have loved to want us to be like Him, our creator. And in Genesis 3:8 "And they heard the sound of the Lord God walking in the garden in the cool of the day..." (AMP). Why do you think God was there? He was there to fellowship and have communion with His creation, man; the creation He made in his own image.

What do you see through the windows of your heart, when you read, "God so greatly loved and dearly prized the world that He (even) gave up His only begotten (unique) Son, so that whoever believes in (trusts in, clings to, relies on) Him shall not perish (come to destruction, be lost) but have eternal (everlasting) life." "For God did not send the Son into the world in order to judge *Wow, in His Holy Image.* (to reject, to condemn, to pass sentence on) the world, but that the world might find salvation and be made safe and sound through Him." John 3:16-17 (AMP). Most of us can attest, that this verse, John 3:16 was probably in the top three of the first we memorized. But somehow, many of us didn't read on. We stopped there. Together, let's read on, "He who believes in Him (who clings to, trusts in, relies on Him) is not judged (he who trusts in Him never comes up for judgment; for him there is no rejection, no condemnation– he incurs no damnation): but he who does not believe (cleave to, rely on, trust

111

in Him) is judged already (he has already been convicted and has already received his sentence) because he has not believed in and *Jesus is Love.* trusted in the name of the only begotten Son of God. (He is condemned for refusing to let his trust rest in Christ's name)." John 3:18 (AMP).

What are you trusting in today? Is it a romance, a career, a child, a house, a parent? Where have you placed your confidence and trust?

Webster's definition of trust reads like this: reliance on the integrity, ability, of a person or thing. Confident; expectation; hope; one upon which a person relies, something entrusted to one's care.

Where is your hope, your expectation, your reliance, and your confidence?

Jesus is the only One who will never forsake or leave you. He has the power to help you in your time of need.

What's love? An even better definition of love than that of Webster is the name of JESUS. God's love is deeper than even Mr. Webster can describe.

The Almighty Creator who walked in the cool of the day with His beloved Adam; the magnificent Holy One who sits on His throne with Jesus at His right side as our Savior, is the same God who proclaimed, in Jeremiah 31:3 (KJV) "...Yes, I have loved you with an everlasting love; therefore with loving kindness have I drawn you and continued My faithfulness to you." He is saying "I LOVE YOU." He's the same One and only God who tells you in Zephaniah 3:17 (KJV) ..."He will rejoice over thee with singing." Can you imagine that; the holy God actually singing over you?

Let's camp out here for a few minutes. These are love notes to us. Let's ponder these words. Everlasting. We don't hear that word often do we? In a world where the secular and Christian world alike is experiencing divorce at a staggering rate, it's hard to comprehend everlasting.

Could it be this love of God is even greater than the love a man and woman have for each other? Absolutely, no comparison. God can't lie. (Hebrews 6:18) His word says "everlasting". He has so much joy over us, He actually sings over us. Now *Become as a little child.* tell me, when was the last time someone sang over you?

In Matthew 18:3 (AMP), Jesus said, "Truly I say to you, unless you repent (change, turn about) and become like little children (trusting, lowly, loving, forgiving) you can never enter the kingdom of heaven (at all)." Is it not time to become as a little child and give our hearts to the real Father, instead of the imitator? Why is it so hard for us to repent? We have a Savior who is not condemning, who never says, "I told you so." He loves us lavishly. He did everything for us. He made it so easy. And all He asked from us in return is to turn from wickedness and turn to Him. Return to His adoring, extravagant love.

We can't compare Jesus' love to anyone on earth. It's like trying to compare a swimming pool to the ocean. Both have water and both have depth; You can swim in them. But the swimming pool can get a leak and the water will be gone. It will not have enough water in it to hold you up, but did you ever see a leak in the ocean? You never fear running out of water there. Jesus' love is deeper than the ocean. (Romans 8:39) I remember once I worked with a young man who had a son eighteen months old. The young son was running around the house with a cup about one-fourth full of orange juice. The young Dad tried to take the cup away from the small child to fill his cup back up, but as soon as Dad took the cup away from the child, his son started to cry, kick and scream. He continued reaching for the cup. A tug of war between the two began. The Dad gently explained to his young son, "Stop crying, I'm not taking your cup away, I'm trying to give you more. Son, I'm trying to fill up your cup." Does this sound familiar? Sometimes we

I'm trying to give you more.

try so hard to hold on to a little bit instead of letting go and allowing Jesus to fill our cup.

I think we're beginning to understand that He is saying, "Come." Just "come". Come and drink the living water. Isn't it about now, that your spirit and soul and mind are crying out? "O, Lord you are worthy to receive the glory and the honor and the power, for you have created all things. They were created and called into being by your act of will." Rev. 4:11 (CLB).

Won't you ask Him today to be first in your heart and life? Today, fall in love with Jesus. He's awesomely in love with you; don't you want to love Him too? If you don't know how, ask Him to teach you how. When Jesus rose from the grave we know Mary's voice rang out as she finally realized it was her Savior who had risen from the grave. She called out "Raboni." Teacher. Ask Him to teach you to love Him more. He tells us in Deuteronomy 4:29, "But if from there you will seek (inquire for and require as necessity) the Lord your God, you will find Him if you (truly) seek Him with all your heart (and mind) and soul and life." (AMP).

Come and drink the living water.

Seek Him first and all other things will be added. Love Him first and you won't love others less, you'll just love Him more.

Our Father desires a love relationship with you. I can remember at one point in my life, my experiences of joy and smelling the roses were hurried moments in time. My Savior was calling with a plan but I was so busy executing "My Plan", I didn't have time to listen. My Savior rarely got all of me, even in church, since my mind was so busy planning the next day. I remember well one day when the *I had idols in my life.* Father spoke to my heart and made me aware that I had idols in my life. At first I denied, with "Oh, no". But quickly I began to realize how much time I spent on my career, the love for my family and my precious children and what little time I spent sharing with God and reading His Word. How seldom my thoughts turned to Him unless I was in trouble. My family and career were on the throne God belonged on, and I had put them there.

One day, I calculated the time I spent thinking about my family with the amount of time I spent thinking about God then tearfully I confessed this to our Father. I knew He wasn't first in my life. I told Him I wanted to love Him more, but I didn't know how. I asked Him to teach me to love Him more. Almost immediately, praise music came into my life. I developed a great hunger and thirst for his Word. I would sometimes come in from work and began cooking dinner, stirring with my left hand and

116

turning pages of the Bible with my right. As my family asked what was going on, I explained; I had asked the Father to help me love Him first in my life. And He was drawing me. I remember so well the day I realized that I truly did love Him with all my heart, my soul and my might.

The most amazing thing happened, I didn't love my family less; I just loved Jesus more. The wonderful thing about our Lord is He meets us just where we are. We don't have to fix things first.

Hebrews 4:15-16 tells us, "We don't have a priest who is out of touch with our reality. He's been through weakness and testing, experienced it all –all but the sin. So let's walk right up to him and get what he is so ready to give. Take the mercy, accept the help." (The message)

So, let us do as Hebrews 4:16 tells us, "Let us then fearlessly and confidently and boldly draw near to the throne of grace (the throne of God's unmerited favor to us sinners), that we may receive mercy (for our failures) and find grace to help in good time for every need (appropriate help and well-timed help, coming just when we need it.)" (AMP). Thank you sweet Jesus.

I just loved Jesus more.

Isn't it time to say, Lord, I give up? Here's my one-fourth cup, I so much want to trade it in on your overflowing cup. I want to be willing to receive Your ravishing love.

He tells us to fearlessly approach the throne, the throne of grace. Do you ever wonder what it looks like there?

Who can go to the throne?   Hebrews 4:16 says, "So let us come boldly to the very throne of *Who can go to the throne?* God and stay there to receive His mercy and to find grace to help us in our times of need." (CLB). Jesus sits at his right hand.   He is able to save completely anyone who comes to the throne. He will remind God that He paid for our sins with His blood. No sin is too big. Now here comes the most absolute, incredible discovery. The heavenly hosts call him "Lord, God Almighty." In Matt. 6:9, Jesus taught us to pray addressing Him as Father. In Rom. 8:15-17, we are told after we accept Jesus as our Savior, we are the adopted children of God. We are His children! We can call him Abba, Father, which means Daddy. I love the way Mike Bickle tells in his book "Passion for Jesus", what happens when we pray. Mike says, he visualizes Jesus at the right hand of God, illuminating in all His splendor, perhaps smilingly motioning us to approach Him. Here comes the most awesome, magnificent sight. The mighty throngs of angels are parting to let you through, for they step aside softly when they see a child of God approaching the throne. Isn't that the most incredible image you've ever seen in your life? And He says, "Come, Come to Abba Father." Come to Daddy; tell me what is on your mind.

Nothing can happen until you believe. Let's see what Webster says about believe: Believe, is to accept the truth, existence, reliability, or value of something. Jesus did the hard part. Our part is to just "come" and drink the living waters. Our part is to believe.

Don't be robbed of reading your Love Letter. How many of you have kept love letters and read them over and over? Women hide them in the jewelry boxes and in shoeboxes on a shelf in their closet.

How many stories have we heard of soldiers in trenches, in the heat of battle pulling out that love letter to read it one more time! *"come" and drink the living waters.* The Bible is your Love Letter. When I taught children's Sunday school classes, I learned to appreciate the simplicity of the Children's Living Bible. I, still read it to this day. I learned to hear God by reading the Amplified version, which clarifies the original Greek and Hebrew language, and to appreciate the poetic splendor by reading the

King James Version. Just pick one translation and begin reading your Love Letter today.

Never before in the history of time have people been busier, rushing to and fro. It is nothing for people to hold two, sometimes three jobs. We never seem to get all the reading done that we plan to do.

Let's hear what God says about that. He tells us in Psalm 127:2-3, "It is useless to get up early and stay up late in order to earn a living. God takes care of his own, even while they sleep." (The Promise) I can relate to this so well, as I too was a working mother of three children. It seemed no matter how early I got up or how late I stayed up, my work was never finished. I failed to make time

There's something missing in my life.

to study my Lord's Love Letter to me, His Word, the Bible, and I'm sure it saddened Him to see me so frustrated, never feeling good about myself, always knowing there was something lacking.

The thought intruded into my mind more times than I care to admit, "I love my family, but I just can't seem to get everything done. There is something missing in my life. I'm so busy. So I left out, the very missing ingredient that was my answer. I left out reading the Bible. I smile sadly now because I was quite a distance runner, running from God and not even realizing I was running. You see, I was going through the motions. After all, I did always attend church. It was what all good people do. Right? I very much wanted to be a "good" person. I just left out the most important part of all; the relationship. Have you ever tried to have a relationship with someone and never talked with them? It's impossible isn't it? I left out my prayer life and reading my Love Letter from God. There were so many things I was *" doing it my way."* frustrated about. God had the answers for me in His Word, but I was so busy "doing it my way," that I didn't take time to pray about it or read God's instruction book.

Our Father is a Gentleman. Even though He yearns for His children, He doesn't intrude. But if we draw near to Him He'll draw near to us.

Our Love Letter from God tells us that as long as we are on earth we will have trials and tribulations. Rain falls on the just and the unjust.

Did you ever have a broken heart? "The Lord is close to those whose hearts are breaking; he rescues those who are humbly sorry for their sins." Psalm 34:18 (CLB) "Come". Come and experience His lavish love. Come and experience Psalm 34:8 (CLB). "Protect me as you would the pupil of your eye; hide me in the shadow of your wings as you hover over me." You can't get much more care than someone protecting their eyes can you?

I have experienced Psalm 18:16 (CLB) "He reached down from heaven and took me and drew me out of my great trials. He rescued me from deep waters. He delivered me from my strong enemy, from those who hated me – I who was helpless in their hands." Remember, our Father, is no respecter of persons. (Acts 10:34) What He does for one, He will do for all that believe and trust in Him.

I remember that my youngest son Tony once owned a bright red T-shirt when he was about four. *He can't take His eyes off of me.* In bright yellow and blue letters, it said, "Jesus loves me so much, He can't take His eyes off of me." It was his favorite shirt and mine too. We loved it so much that we had to wash it often. The red turned to a faded pink color. When his navel started to show, we knew it had reached its season. Nowhere could we find another one just like it. Now, it gently reminds me why we loved it so.

Our Father tells us, in Psalm 140:15, "You were there while I was being formed in utter seclusion! You saw me before I began to breathe. Every day was recorded in your book!" (CLB). I remember that I recorded every little detail in my children's baby books; how much they weighed, how long they were, their first smile and when they first rolled over. Our dear Father has recorded our every day. Ponder this: if our Father loved us so much to record our every day, to actually tattoo our pictures on the palm of His hand (Isaiah 49:16), number the hairs on our head, (Matthew 10:30), then end the day singing over us. (Zeph. 3:17) Why would we ignore Him? Why wouldn't we want to just take a few moments to just "bask in His love"?

A couple of years ago, I attended a ladies mentoring conference in Denver, Colorado. Due to my flight arrangements, I arrived a whole day ahead of time. There was a car rental in the hotel where I was staying, so after I learned I was very close to Vail, Colorado, I decided to spend the day experiencing God's beauty. As I pulled out from the hotel parking lot, I prayed, "Ok, Father, it's just You and me. Show me Your splendor." It was one of the most delightful days of my life. Around every curve was a new experience, a breathtaking view of my Lord's creation. As I pulled onto the interstate, I breathed a prayer to our Father, "Show me Your handiwork." It seemed around every curve I encountered the mountains just got bigger and more majestic. It was as if the Prince of Peace was my guide. It was as if He had

I could almost feel His breath on my cheek.

planned this magnificent surprise for me. I could hear Him say, "You've not seen anything yet." And He was right. The scenery was stunning; the conversation was heavenly. The majesty of the mountains and the light spirit of the small village at the base of the mountain were so inspiring. As I stopped and had lunch, I talked with the Father. To others I was alone, but I was never more fulfilled with His presence. He was so close I could almost feel His breath on my cheek. It was as if He was showing His daughter around. After all, isn't that what every child wants; a whole day with her Father? My heart was in awe and as He and I walked through the flower garden and experienced the splendor of His magnificent beauty and creation. It was as if I could hear Him say, "Wait till you see what I plan to show you next." That night in my hotel room as I turned off the light, I prayed, "Father, what a wonderful day I've had with you. Thank you for your love and mercy." He is no respecter of persons. He's the perfect Father; He has no favorites. What He did for me that day in Vail, He wants to do with each of His children.

He is no respecter of persons.

Jesus wants to share in our fun days too, our days of play. We so often, don't spend time with God until we are in trouble. "Jesus help me." "God help me." He wants us to call out to Him when we are in trouble. Psalm 91:15 (NIV). "He shall call upon Me, and I will answer him; I will be with him in trouble, I will deliver him and honor him." Ruth Bell Graham tells a story of a poor woman who went up to the foothills of a Chinese town to cut the grass. Her baby was tied to her back and a little child walked beside her. In her hand was a sickle. Just as she reached the top of a hill, she heard a roar. Frightened, she turned and saw a tigress springing at her, followed by her two cubs. The illiterate Chinese woman had never attended school or church, but a missionary had once told her about Jesus, "Who is able to help you when you are in trouble." As the tiger's claws tore into her arm, the woman cried out, "O Jesus, help me!" The tiger, instead of attacking again, suddenly turned and ran away. The Bible says, "He will give his angels charge concerning you to guard you in all your ways." Psalm 91:11 (NAS) He will be there for us. But how about a day, like mine in late October in Vail, Colorado, just an ordinary Thursday. He wants to be with you, showing you His handiwork.

"O Jesus, help me!"

Think on this. Our dear Father, through David, tells us, in Psalm 139:17-18 (CLB) "How precious it is, Lord, to realize that you are thinking about me constantly! I can't even count how many times a day your thoughts turn towards me, and when I awaken in the morning you are still thinking about me!" Father, "Search me, O God, and know my heart; test my thoughts. Point out anything you find in me that makes you sad, and lead me along the path of everlasting life." Psalm 139:23 (CLB). Is it as hard for you to comprehend, as it is for me that our precious Father is constantly thinking about us? How much do you think God loves Jesus? Jesus is His only begotten Son. Well, in John 17:23 He tells us He loves us just like He loves Jesus. In 1 John 4:16 we learn that God is not distant and angry but the complete expression of love. God is love.

"Search me, oh God, and know my heart."

Have you ever had a promise made to you that was broken?   Well, God is a promise keeper. He tells us in Psalm 146:6 (CLB), that He is the God who keeps promises. When we put our faith in man, even the greatest leaders fail, for every man must die. His breathing stops, life ends, and in a moment all he planned for himself is ended. But happy is the man who has the God of Jacob as his helper, whose hope is in the Lord his God.

Who or what do we have our faith in that is worth giving up a real, love relationship with Jesus? Are you running from God? God is everywhere; you can't run. Ask God to give you a willing heart. In

Psalm 119:32, it is written, "I will (not merely walk) but run the way of your commandments, when You give me a heart that is willing." (AMP). Ask Him to grant you a heart that is willing.

Psalm 141:1-4, says, " QUICK LORD, ANSWER me--for I have prayed. Listen when I cry to you for help! Regard my prayer as my evening sacrifice and as incense wafting up to you. Help me Lord, to keep my mouth shut and my lips sealed." (AMP). Ever pray that one? I like David, have prayed that many times. God wants to speak to us even more that we want to hear Him. He speaks through His Word, circumstances and, yes, sometimes through other people.

Are you weary from *trying*? Weary from *trying* to succeed? Worn out from *trying* to be a good mother, *trying* to be a good wife, *trying* to excel in your career, weary, bone-tired? He says, "Come unto me all ye that labour and are heavy laden, and I will give you rest." (Matthew 11:28) (KJV). He is the answer. Jesus is *God loves sinners.* generous with His forgiveness. God loves sinners. (I Timothy 1:15) He showers unconditional forgiveness. This is urgent, listen closely: Isaiah 55:6, "Seek the Lord while you can find Him. Call on him now while he is near." (NLT). You see, the devil is clever and his response to you is "Wait, think this over, wait, another day might be better."

But in our Love Letter from God, the Bible, Ecclesiastes 11:4 says, "Those who wait for perfect weather will never plant seeds; those who look at every cloud will never harvest crops. In the same way, you don't know what God is doing. You don't know where the wind will blow, and you don't know how a baby grows inside the mother. In the same way, you don't know what God is doing, or how he created everything." (NCV). Ecclesiastes 3:11..."God does everything just right and on time." (NCV). He is never tardy. And today is the time. Jesus' invitation is "Come." Don't delay.

Won't you ask Him today? He's lavishly in love with you; don't you want to love Him too? Remember, when you ask Him to teach you to love Him first in your life, your life will never be the same. Father, I know you are the lover of my soul.

In I Peter 2:24, the Word says, "He personally carried the load of our sins in his own body when he died on the cross, so that we can be finished with sin and live a good life from now on. For His wounds have healed ours. (25) Like sheep you wandered away from God, but now you have returned to your Shepherd, the Guardian of your souls who keeps you safe from all attacks." (CLB). Open up your heart to God and listen very carefully.

Another way of saying this is in Isaiah 53:4-6, "Yet it was our grief He bore, our sorrows that weighed Him down. And we thought His troubles were a punishment from God, for His own sins! (5) But He was wounded and bruised for our sins. He was chastised that we might have peace; He was lashed-- and we were healed! (6) We are the ones that strayed away like sheep! We, who left God's paths to follow our own. Yet God laid on Him the guilt and sins of every one of us!" (CLB). May we have the grace and mercy to run, not walk, straight into the arms of our Savior. Children of God, look up and search for Him with all your heart. He tells us in Deuteronomy 4:29, "But if from there you will seek (inquire for and require as necessity) the Lord, your God, you will find Him if you (truly) seek Him with all your heart (and mind) and soul and life." (AMP).

Look up and search for Him with all your heart.

Once again, I make reference to Mike Bickle in his book "Passion for Jesus". He shared that when he began praying it felt like he was praying to the air. He didn't feel connected so he tried gazing on the throne. Just as A.W. Tozer once suggested, we need to practice the long and loving meditation upon the majesty of God. I take it one step further, I don't just gaze on the throne, I "bask in the love from the throne." Pray Ephesians 1:17 over yourself. Ask God, the glorious Father of Jesus Christ, to give you wisdom to see clearly and really understand who Christ is and all that He has done for you.   Read John 17:27. Pray asking God the Father to help you love Jesus as God the Father loves Jesus.

It's no wonder skepticism creeps in when we live on an earth, where, when a child dies, often the first suspect is the mother or the dad, where our whole system cries out "What's in it for me?" In a system that we are taught there are no *"and a two edged sword in their hands."* free lunches. Nothing's for Free. It's no wonder that we can barely comprehend a Father, a majestic King, taking off His crown and His robe and storming the gates of Hell to come after us, with never a thought of what's in it for Him. He is driven by love. Divine love. Agape love. It's a love we can't understand but hopefully from glory to glory He will teach us to love with that kind of love and He will teach us to run into His arms to receive His free gift of Jesus.

Psalm 149:6, "Let the high praises of God be in their throats and a two-edged sword in their hands." (AMP). Father, in Hebrews 4:12, you tell us that, "For the Word that you speak is alive and full

130

of power, it is sharper than any two edged sword penetrating the soul, dividing the soul, and the spirit, and the deepest parts of our nature, exposing, shifting, analyzing and judging the very thoughts and purposes of our hearts." (AMP), In Rev. 1:16, You tell us... "and from His mouth there came forth a sharp two-edged sword, and His face was like the sun shining in full power at midday." (AMP).

Precious Father, You tell us in Psalm 150:1 "PRAISE THE LORD! Praise God in His sanctuary; praise Him in the heavens of His power! (2) Praise Him for His mighty acts; praise Him according to the abundance of His greatness! (6) Let everything that has breath and every breath of life praise the Lord! Praise the Lord! (Hallelujah!)" (AMP). And amen.

Precious children of God accept His mercy and His grace and run into His arms from where you are. If you're just beginning your journey, then ask Him into your heart. If you've started your journey and decided to go back, set your face like flint, turn, and lock gazes with Him. Look deep into His Word and know you are loved, you are received and *Come just as you are.* you are forgiven. Come, just as you are. Change your course and head toward Home. I know many of you are beat up, battle scarred, tired, discouraged, disillusioned, and wounded. I too, have been there. Turn your eyes on Jesus, and look into His wonderful face. He won't browbeat you, scold you, or say, "I told you so." Our Savior's eyes are always sweeping the earth looking for that willing heart. He'll see you from afar. He'll leave His throne, come out and meet you running with your ring and your robe and sandals, calling over his shoulder to put the grain fattened calf on to roast. His precious

"What's love? In Heaven, it's your name."

child is coming home. He tells us in Luke 15:7, "I tell you that in the same way, there will be more joy in heaven over one sinner who repents than over ninety-nine righteous persons who need no repentance." (10) "In the same way there is joy in the presence of the angels of God when one sinner repents." (NAS).

Precious child of God, a party is in the making in Heaven and I hear they are whispering your name. What's love? In Heaven, it's your name. Did you not know, my friend, you are the child of a King? And He loves you so much He can't take His eyes off of **you**.

Father, lover of my soul, I have sinned against You. I want forgiveness for all my sins. I believe that Jesus died on the cross for me and rose again. Father, I give You my life to do with as You wish. I need Your love and forgiveness. I want Jesus to come into my life and into my heart, and forgive my sins and give me eternal life with You. This I ask in Jesus name.

Father, draw me unto You. Teach me Raboni to love You, as I should. Teach me Your ways. We know that everything that You have made, gives praise to You. Your glory is greater than all the heavens. Father, You love a humble, contrite heart. Help us to be humble servants and have contrite hearts.

Father, grant us hearts that are willing and a heart that is after You. Help us, Father, to love what You love and to hate what You hate.

Grant us, Father, the ability to love others, as You would have us do.

Anoint us from the heavens Father; anoint us from the holy throne room, anoint us Father with Your love. In Jesus' name I pray,

With Love,

Gloria

Ask Jesus Into Your Life To Be Lord And Savior

Romans 8-11, "The Word that saves is right here, as near as the tongue in your mouth, as close as the heart in your chest." It's the word of faith that welcomes God to go to work and set things right for us. This is the core of our preaching. Say the welcoming word to God—"Jesus is my Master"—embracing, body and soul, God's work of doing in us what he did in raising Jesus from the dead. That's it. You're not "doing" anything; you're simply calling out to God, trusting Him to do it for you. That's salvation. With your whole being you embrace God setting things right, and then you say it, right out loud: "God has set everything right between him and me!" Scripture reassures us, "No one who trusts God like this--heart and soul—will ever regret it." (The Message)

Dear Father,

I have sinned against You. I want forgiveness for all my sins. I believe that Jesus died on the cross for me and rose again. Father, I give my life to do with as You wish. I need your love and forgiveness. I want Jesus to come into my life and into my heart. This I ask in Jesus' name.

Write to us and we will send you information to start you on your journey with Christ.

God's Glorious Grace Ministries
4013 Clearwater Way
Lexington, Ky. 40515
859-245-7771

About the Author

Gloria Coffelt resides in Lexington, KY, with her husband, Gary. She has three sons, Scott, Tony, and Jeff (Jennifer), and twin grandchildren, Jake and Jensen, whom Gloria often refers to as her "little blessings."

She is the founder of "God's Glorious Grace Ministries." A 1996 graduate of Christian Leaders and Speakers Seminars (CLASS), led by author and speaker Florence Littauer, Gloria is a national speaker at conferences and retreats for "seeking" women. She also has held ladies seminars in St. Petersburg, Russia. "Dear Lord, With Love, Gloria", was previously translated into Russian and distributed in 1996. Gloria is presently writing a second work entitled "May I See Them Through Your Eyes." It comes as a result of the author's extensive career travel, which allowed her to witness God's majestic, incredible power in the marketplace.

While serving as a Regional Vice-President with a mid-size insurance company Gloria felt the gentle, yet persuasive call from the Heavenly Father into a women's Christian speaking ministry. She responded, "Yes Lord, send me."

The speaker has many stories, and prayers to share via a unique ability to take her listeners along to experience God's awesome presence and love. In one moment, you'll be caught up in laughter and in the next, shed a tear. Gloria is energized and with her love for all people, appeals to any age. She will gently remind you that God has no favorites, but that you are His Special, beloved child.

Gloria, is involved in outreach and evangelism through Southland Christian Church in Lexington, Ky.

Resources

Mike Bickle, "Passion for Jesus", Creation House Publishers, 1993

A.W. Tozer, "The Knowledge of the Holy", Harper Collins Publishers, 1992

Ruth Graham, story about the Chinese woman

Margaret Therkelsen, "The Love Exchange", Fleming H. Revell, division of Baker Book House Co., Grande Rapids, MI 49516-6287, www.bakerbooks.com previously published by Bristol Books.

Order Form

Ship to: (Please Print)

NAME:_____

ADDRESS:_____

CITY_____**STATE**_____ **ZIP**_____

DAYTIME PHONE_____ _____-_____

_____**No. Copies @ $ 12.95 ea.** = **$**_____

Postage & Handling @ $2.50 P/book   _____

Kentucky residents add 6% tax   _____

TOTAL AMOUNT ENCLOSED   **$** _____
(Check or money order only)

Make checks payable to:
Gloria Coffelt

Send to: Gloria Coffelt
4013 Clearwater Way
Lexington, Ky. 40515